REDWOOD
CURTAIN

REDWOOD CURTAIN

A Play

LANFORD WILSON

A Dramabook
HILL and WANG
The Noonday Press
NEW YORK

Copyright © 1993 by Lanford Wilson
All rights reserved
Published simultaneously in Canada by HarperCollins*CanadaLtd*
Printed in the United States of America
Designed by Tere LoPrete

ISBN 0-8090-8052-4

For Rod Marriott

With grateful thanks to Michael Baird, David Kahn, Don Speziale, Lisa Gayton, Rich Remedios, Seattle Rep, Circle Rep Playwrights Lab and the usual suspects: Michael, Marshall, Fred, Claris, Debra, Tanya and Loren Dunlap forever for the Rubber Squirrel.

Redwood Curtain received its world premiere in the Circle Repertory Company production at the Seattle Repertory Theatre on January 8, 1992. It was directed by Marshall W. Mason, with a cast of David Morse as Lyman, Kimiko Cazanov as Geri, and Debra Monk as Geneva.

The Circle Repertory production was next presented by the Philadelphia Drama Guild in association with the Annenberg Center on March 6, 1992. The production in Philadelphia was also directed by Marshall W. Mason, with one change: Lyman was played by Steve Bassett.

Circle Repertory Company is the recipient of a grant award for New American Plays from the W. Alton Jones Foundation supporting the development and production of *Redwood Curtain*.

REDWOOD CURTAIN

CHARACTERS

LYMAN FELLERS is thirty-eight, a veteran of the Vietnam War. He is a large, strong man. He has a stubble of beard and long unkempt hair.

GERI RIORDAN is a seventeen-year-old Asian-American girl. She may be a little more than the eighty-eight pounds she claims, but she is small. She has long black hair. She is quite straightforward, sure of herself, and totally American.

GENEVA SIMONSON is in her mid-forties, smart, well spoken, and a little Western.

THE SCENE

Scene 1: A redwood forest near Arcata, California, in the northwestern part of the state

Scene 2: Briefly a car. The music room of Geneva's home in Arcata

Scene 3: A coffee house, the forest, the music room

TIME

Late June 1990

Redwood Curtain should be performed without intermission.

SCENE 1

A forest of extremely large first-growth redwoods.

LYMAN is a large, strong man with a stubble of beard and longish, unkempt hair. He wears two pairs of pants and two sweaters over a shirt. He carries a knapsack. He is unwashed. His voice is low and raspy, rather rough. He seldom smiles and never laughs. His eyes, while alert, are dull. He is thirty-eight.

A dog is yelping excitedly, chasing a rabbit in the distance.

LYMAN
(Yelling encouragement)
Go go go go! Get him! Catch that mother!
(He drops his knapsack to the ground)
Useless bitch. Better be a damn moose, both of us eat.
(He sits, then yells again)
Stop yappin', bitch. Do it!
(To himself)
Don't come whining back here.
(After a moment GERI, an Asian-American girl of seventeen, can be seen, as far away as possible, silently watching LYMAN. How long has she been there? She moves closer now. She is in a position where she can be seen, but he gives no indication of her presence. GERI is small, straightforward, and totally American)

5

GERI

Excuse me.
>*(Beat)*

Could you tell me where the path is?
>*(She watches him a moment. Nothing)*

If you could just indicate the general direction back to
civilization. I've got myself turned around here.
>*(Pause)*

Mister?
>*(Pause. LYMAN begins digging in his knapsack for
>something; he seems to have withdrawn into
>himself)*

I know you can talk, I heard you yelling to your dog.
>*(She stays some distance from him. From the other
>direction the dog has begun yelping again)*

LYMAN

>*(Jumping up, yelling)*

Get him, get to it, bitch, go!
>*(He sits back down)*

GERI

>*(After a moment)*

What's his name?

LYMAN

You got a dollar?

GERI

What?

LYMAN

You got a dollar on you?

GERI

No, I don't. What a great turnoff. That really says get
out of my face, doesn't it? That must be effective. I didn't

6

bring any money with me this morning. I was just going for a walk. I made the mistake of losing the path. I thought I saw a banana slug. They're supposed to be thick up here, I haven't seen one. Then I kept going like an idiot and got a little lost.

    (Beat)

If you can be a little lost. If you could just point—

LYMAN

You ask the wrong questions. Little girl. Hang on to that purse, must be something in it.

GERI

Yeah, well, my whole life is in it, but I didn't bring any money. Really. It's just I have this terrible sense of direction. I mean, it isn't difficult finding your way *into* the woods, but . . .

    (This dumb place)

I tried looking for moss. It's supposed to grow on the north side of trees, you can use it like a compass. Unfortunately, it's so wet up here the moss grows all the way around the trees. One for the moss.

They have a postcard at the Student Center with the sun shining straight into the woods horizontally that they call "Dawn in the Redwoods," but it's obviously sunset because the sun doesn't come out till about two in the afternoon. If the fog manages to burn off at all. If we're lucky.

    (Pause. She is looking up into the trees, leaning against one)

They're something else, though, aren't they? They're amazing. I wouldn't have believed it. I keep leaning up against them, maybe I'll draw some strength from them. Or perspective. Something. Whatever it is they have. I don't think it's working. This forest is over twenty thousand years old. These trees were standing here when

7

Egypt built pyramids in the Valley of the Kings. They were already the oldest living thing on earth when Jesus was born.

(The hound, way off, begins yapping again)

Which kinna makes me feel, hey, you know, great. One for the redwood. But, I mean, we're taking early retirement at fifty-five? Thanks a lot. We're getting our revenge, though. They're all coming down. This whole place is being bought out. They're all going to be decks and lawn furniture.

LYMAN

(Jumping up, yelling after the dog)

Give up, bitch! You're beat! He's got ya! Pitch it, bitch!

(GERI has started at his sudden movement. He sits back down)

GERI

(After a moment)

Then I realized I don't know which direction Arcata is from here. I mean north, south, east, or west. So it wouldn't have been much help to have a compass. It might have kept me from going around in circles.

In a labyrinth you're supposed to take *every turn* and always turn left and you'll find your way out. I can't wait to try it. That's the sort of knowledge that doesn't help you when you're lost in a redwood forest. Wow! I love the sound of that. Redwood forest. I mean, this is the first time I've seen one. Also the first time I've been lost in one.

(Beat)

One for one.

LYMAN

You won't find your way out from here. You're gonna die here.

8

GERI

(Beat)

Well, okay. I guess that's possible. There's always a first time for everything.

> *(LYMAN has found a package of Bamboo papers in his knapsack. He begins rolling a joint)*

Actually, it wouldn't be the first time. I was in a bike accident when I was twelve. One of my neighbors gave me a joyride on his Harley and ran us into the side of a truck carrying cantaloupes. I think he'd been trying to impress his girlfriend. Apparently it worked, she married him. I was on the operating table for seven hours. My spine and left hip were partially crushed. Only when they gave me the anesthetic my heart stopped for twenty-two seconds.

I didn't see the Terrible Bright White Light at the End of the Tunnel.

> *(She shrugs)*

Everybody asks. Sometimes I say I did, because when I say I didn't they think I wasn't really dead. I asked my doctor if I really was dead for twenty-two seconds and he said you really were dead for twenty-two seconds. So I asked him for a death certificate, but he wouldn't give me one.

(Beat)

All these malpractice suits probably.

(Beat)

I imagine you saw a lot of that, huh?

(Beat)

Death.

LYMAN

Shit.

GERI

Yeah. Are you gonna light that joint or what?

> *(As she starts to reach for the joint, LYMAN makes*

9

a grab for her purse. GERI *jumps aside. There is a
flash of lightning, a roll of thunder.* LYMAN *looks
around him in dismay)*

Hey, you! Watch it! Come on, guy! I'd as soon break
your arm as shake your hand. I can take care of myself.
(Quickly improvising)
I mean, uh . . . I'm a black belt in karate.

LYMAN

Never tell your opponent what he's up against.

GERI

Yeah, well, I believe in fair warning.

LYMAN

Don't show your hand.

GERI

Just believe it.

LYMAN

What do you want from me?

GERI

Listen, I was just on a little expedition to look at the
plant life. I study botany. Most of this stuff I've never
seen before.

LYMAN

Bullshit. I thought you were looking for slugs.

GERI

We don't have redwoods where I live. Or ferns like
these. I know their botanical name, I just can't remember it right now. I only know them from these pressed-
like specimens we have in class.

LYMAN

You always carry your purse in the woods?

GERI

It was a spur-of-the-moment decision.

LYMAN

You wear sneakers and shorts, dress like that on a hike?

GERI

God, it was a whim! I wasn't planning to rappel mountains or anything.

LYMAN

Who do you think you're talking to?

GERI

I have no idea, I was just—

LYMAN

—With your black belt in karate and your sneakers and shorts. You think I'm deaf? I look blind to you?

GERI

I'm not really putting together what it is that you're trying to say.

LYMAN

You been following me for the last two hours!
    (A long pause)

GERI

Well, you were yelling, I could hardly keep from hearing you.

11

LYMAN

I was standing on G Street, you came out of your yogurt milk-shake shop, you followed me a mile up 101, you followed me into the trees, you followed me along the dry creek, you followed me up the hill, you followed me around the fern valley. Now you're lost, aren't you? You don't know where the fuck you are.

GERI

Well, just because I say something, actually, doesn't necessarily mean I mean it. I mean, I'm a terrible liar.

LYMAN

Nobody can lie to me. You can't be lied to if you don't listen.

GERI

You did listen, though. I can tell.

LYMAN

I don't hear you, so forget it. I don't hear nobody.

GERI
(She takes this quite seriously)
I'll bet you don't, either. What do you hear?

LYMAN

They got all you college jerks looking in the woods for everybody's plants. Get your neck broke for you, is what you'll get.

GERI

I don't believe I know what you're saying.

LYMAN

You're not dumb. Come in here, think I'm gonna lead
you to something. Come back and pull up my plants.
Turn in my name. Just go on.

GERI

Oh, I'm with you. You're talking contraband. I don't
want your marijuana plants, if that's what you're saying.
They'll have to legalize it eventually.

LYMAN

You in school here?

GERI

They're supposed to have one of the best horticulture
departments in the country. Fruit trees and all that. It's
a little agrarian for what I want, but I figure I'll go two
years and transfer.

LYMAN

Let me see your ID.

GERI

My what?

LYMAN

Your school ID.

GERI

Back at the dorm.

LYMAN

Throw it over here.

GERI

I don't have it on me.

LYMAN

Give it here, damnit.

GERI

I'm not carrying it, I said. Jesus.

LYMAN

If you don't give me your school ID, I'm gonna take the thing away from you.

GERI

You don't frighten me.

LYMAN

(Getting up)
Throw me your damn purse. Do it!

GERI

(Digging into her purse)
Okay. Just sit down. God.
(She fishes her driver's license out of her wallet)
I feel like I'm being carded.
(She pitches her license to him)
That picture's awful.

LYMAN

(Reading)
California. What's "La Jolly"?

GERI

Well, you're not Spanish. You must belong to the other half of the country's population. La Jolla is a town north of San Diego. I have no idea what it means. It may *mean* "jolly" for all I know. It isn't.

LYMAN

Where's your student ID, Geraldine Lon?

14

GERI

Geri. Only they wouldn't let me put that on the license.

LYMAN

What kind of name is Lon?

GERI

That's my mother's name. Vietnamese. She was going to call me Farrow, which was Dad's name, but she looked it up in the dictionary and it means "to give birth to a litter of pigs."

LYMAN

Toss over the wallet.

GERI

No. I mean it.

LYMAN

What you got from that school?

GERI

Nothing on me.

LYMAN

This isn't you. You're no twenty-one. You don't go to that college either. How old are you?

GERI

I might have gone to school here. I considered it. You look at all of them. You go to these ridiculously over-endowed campuses in the middle of these poverty-stricken redneck towns, decide you wouldn't go there if it were the last school on earth, then they turn you down anyway. What Humboldt is really hot for is land management and conservation, which is something I

15

just like respect the shit out of but it's not me. Could I have my driver's license back?

(A beat. Leveling with him)

I came to Arcata to visit a friend of Mom's, this professor. He teaches here. I'm staying with him and his wife.

LYMAN

What's his name?

GERI

You're familiar with the faculty? Dr. Smith. Really. Mathematics. Only not the interesting stuff; not theory or astrophysics or anything, so he's kinna dry, but his wife is cool.

LYMAN

(He holds up the license)

You make that face on purpose? You thought that was cute?

GERI

We were all goofing. I don't like to have my picture taken.

(Beat)

You should understand that.

LYMAN

Let me see your wallet.

GERI

I'd rather not.

LYMAN

Yeah? Hand it here.

16

GERI

No.

LYMAN

Why not?

GERI

(Beat)
Because it has all the money I have left for my whole
vacation in it.

LYMAN

I could take it away from you.

GERI

No, you can't. You really can't. I can run faster than
you can. Actually, you get around the woods pretty well,
but on 101 I could tell you still limp. When you're hus-
tling the tourists you tell them you got shot up in Cam-
bodia, but really you were passed out in Isaac Minor
Alley and Buzz Warren ran his pickup over your foot.
He started to get out, your dog nearly took his leg off.
Did you know that? He had to drive down to a doctor
in Eureka for stitches. He didn't go to the hospital because he hadn't turned on his lights; since he was sneak-
ing out of the alley after sticking it to Mrs. Reason.
     The police took you to the emergency room, where
you basically freaked. On the local skinny, Mrs. Smith
is very up to speed.

LYMAN

Take out the money and hand over the wallet.

GERI

Except you. That's all she knew about you.
          *(A pause. He hands her the license. As she reaches
          for it he grabs her arm, whirls her around, and*

17

*though she tries several moves he has her down on
her face on the ground with his foot in the middle
of her back)*
You bastard! You're killing me! You're squashing my
breasts, damnit.
*(He takes the wallet from her bag, drops the bag
beside her, and steps off)*
Just take the money and give me the wallet. Don't paw
my things.

LYMAN

(Thumbing through the money)
Jesus Christ, haven't you ever heard of traveler's
checks?

GERI

All the tellers at my bank suck. Now give me my damn
wallet.
*(And she flies at him. There is a huge scuffle during
which she gets in one really solid jab to the gut,
enough to make us believe she might really know
the rudiments of karate, but she ends up face down
in the dirt again with him sitting on her butt)*

LYMAN

Are you gonna act nice? Are you gonna act nice?

GERI

Could you put that some other way?

LYMAN

Are you gonna act nice?

GERI

Sure!
(He gets off her back. She rolls over)
I'm dead.

(Quite angry)
I told you I've got a bad back. I've got a plastic hip and a steel rod in my spine. I can't fight. I weigh eighty-eight pounds. What the hell are you doing? I'm frail, stupid!

LYMAN

I didn't believe you.

GERI

That part was true. I thought you didn't hear people. You were too busy marching to the beat of your own drum or something.

LYMAN
(Beat. He is looking through her wallet)
You got your whole life in here, huh?
(Beat)
I could leave you here, you'd die.

GERI
(Still flushed)
I have an infallible sense of direction. It's uncanny. I'm part cat or something.

LYMAN

Which way is Arcata?

GERI
(She points back and to the right)
About six miles that way. The last hour we've been going around in circles. What, were you trying to confuse me? I thought you were losing it.

LYMAN

You lie about everything?

GERI

The truth isn't all it's cracked up to be. I don't know
how lying got such a bad rap. Could you give me that
back, please? It makes me incredibly nervous to see
someone pawing it. Really.

LYMAN

I don't believe your reallys anymore.

GERI

You are such a total troll. I was embarrassed following
you, the way you stomp through the woods like a rhino
or something. You don't even feel the enchantment, do
you? I probably should teach you a lesson. You've lim-
ited yourself to such a physical, blundering oafdom that
you can actually sit talking to a sylph and not even know
it.

LYMAN

A what?

GERI

A nymph, a sylph. Actually, more of a genie.

LYMAN

In shorts and sneakers?

GERI

I just threw something on! You couldn't lose me in the
woods. The deer would guide me out. I could make the
whole woods vanish if I wanted. If I were in danger the
trees would bend down so I could clasp their highest
bough, then they'd swing up and throw me to safety.
I'm just lucky you didn't ask me where I keep my pot
of gold. When we're helpless we're compelled to reveal
its hiding place.

That's a leprechaun.
> *(He holds up a picture from her wallet, just flashing*
> *it. He doesn't take it from its sleeve)*

Who's that?

GERI

Me and a couple of girlfriends. The blonde actually got married last week. Which is like unbelievable because she is the most totally user-friendly girl in my class. To some geek from Bakersfield. And will be living there if you can believe it. I wouldn't have followed you at all if I'd known you'd pull that Rambo macho crap.

LYMAN

What's that?

GERI

Trying to act like some damn Rambo or somebody.

LYMAN

Who's he?

GERI

You can't mean it. I'd willingly trade places with anyone alive who'd never heard that name.

A bullshit Marine in the movies. He's sent back to Nam, like this one-man army, to rescue a group of MIAs. And before he leaves, you'll like this, he says to his captain, "Are they gonna let us win this time?"

The movie house goes wild.

Suddenly everyone in the theater realizes the only way our boys could have lost is if someone wouldn't let them win. We were double-crossed. Have you been away so long you don't know you're a hero now? Come home, all is forgiven. We don't have a Vietnam syndrome anymore. Ollie-Ollie Oxen free. We win. It makes you wonder about all the wonderful wars we won.

LYMAN
(He holds up another photo from the wallet)
Who's that?

GERI
My mother.

LYMAN
Pretty.

GERI
I'll tell her.
(He holds up another and keeps it up)
Do you mind? That's the woman who bought me from my real mother. Not a bad investment, but she has a nose for that sort of thing. I turned out to be this world-class piano prodigy, probably worth a fortune. 'Course she's a billionaire, money means nothing to those people. And if you believe that, she has a bridge she'd like to sell you.
(He continues to hold the photo up)
Her name's Julia. She's my foster mother or adopted mother or whatever you call it. She's my mother, she's just not related to me.

LYMAN
(He goes back to the other woman)
Who's this, then?

GERI
That's my real mother, only I've never met her.

LYMAN
How you going to tell her I said she was pretty?

Okay, I won't. Would you give me that back, please?
(He holds up another. Beat)
Julia's husband. Laird Alfred Leslie Riordan. "Alfred
Leslie" because he claimed to be related to the composer Erik Alfred Leslie Satie. He was my foster father.
Died two years ago. Taught me all the usual parlor
tricks—play an instrument, jump through hoops, roller-
skate. All the stuff that kept people entertained at dinner
parties so he could concentrate on his drinking. He was
the only desk-jockey lieutenant, didn't see a day's fighting, to come completely unglued in the war. Came back
and drank himself totally into the toilet.
(He holds up another)
Boy. Lives across the street.

LYMAN

Your boyfriend?

GERI

It's seriously frowned on for nymphs to get involved with
mortals. It's been known to happen, but the results are
inevitably a disaster.
*(He looks at another photo for a moment, then
holds it up)*

LYMAN

Who's the GI?
(A long pause)

GERI

(Very level)
I think that's you.
(A long silent pause)
You're so small in the picture you can't really tell, can
you? Taken seventeen years ago in Saigon. Private Ray
Farrow. You signed the papers for Mother and me to

get out, letter of intent, whatever, then about when we
got on the boat, you took a train north from San Fran-
cisco. The last time anyone heard from you was four
years ago in Hopland. You weren't carrying an ID, but
they knew you from your description. The sheriff told
you to get out of town. Said you hadn't shaved for a
month, looked like a good candidate for the Redwood
Curtain. Can't mess around in Hopland. That's wine
country. They run a model town.

LYMAN
(A beat. He throws her wallet back to her, rather
roughly)
Not me. I didn't fraternize.

GERI
Is that what they call it.

LYMAN
I didn't go with prostitutes.

GERI
Mother owned a florist shop in Saigon.

LYMAN
Pretty stupid to leave that.

GERI
With me on the way?

LYMAN
Good move.

GERI
They'd have killed her probably. I imagine she'd seen
what they did to those who "fraternized" with the
French. She's probably done well here.

LYMAN

Drives a stiff bargain.

GERI

Shrewd cookie.

LYMAN

Hard as nails.

GERI

Inscrutable.

LYMAN

Where is she now?

GERI

No idea.
          (Pause)

LYMAN

Why me?

GERI

I thought I recognized you.

LYMAN

You even know your dad?

GERI

I thought you recognized me.

LYMAN

Never saw you before.

GERI

Neither has my father. I don't think he knows I exist.
Day before yesterday, I saw you standing on the street

25

with your dog. We passed each other and you looked right into my face. I think you saw it then. I did.

LYMAN

Saw what?

GERI

Look in my eyes.

LYMAN

Come on.

GERI

What's wrong?

LYMAN

I saw that genie stuff over there.

GERI

I come from a very magical culture. Don't look down. What do you see? I control the elements.
(It begins to grow dark)
I can gather the clouds from far out at sea and pile them over these woods. I could call upon the air for violence and destruction.
(It is very dark, lightning flashes, a rolling thunder runs over the woods)
I could will it to rain or thin the turbulence, send the clouds out over the ocean and inform the sun to burn through the fog and warm the earth.
(The sun breaks through the clouds and shines brightly)
I can tell the birds to fly to the trees that surround the vineyards across the valley and leave the woods to the two of us.
(Birds call: a light sifting of dry needles falls as they fly off, their calls fading)

Except for the eagle. He protects me. He'll stay.
    (An eagle calls)
Don't you know whom you're dealing with?
    (The sun continues to shine brightly through the
    redwoods)
What's your name?

                    LYMAN
    (After a pause, still looking at her)
One of your eyes is gray.

                    GERI
Almost blue.

                    LYMAN
One is just a normal gook eye, black. The other one is
gray.

                    GERI
That occurs once in ten million. Same odds as the
lottery.

                    LYMAN
With mixed blood you're liable to get anything.

                    GERI
And you. Your eyes are dull, aren't they? They've seen
a lot, haven't they? But it's still discernible. One of your
eyes is blue and the other is brown.

                    LYMAN
Not so anybody would notice.

                    GERI
Americans don't look each other in the eye, for all our
straightforwardness. You'd have to be close to see it. I
did.

LYMAN
You consider yourself American?

GERI
You kidding? I was adopted into one of the Former Top
Ten Families of California. I just don't know where I
was born. Somewhere in the Old Country. To an es-
tranged mother and a father wandering around Eureka,
California, in the fog. With one blue eye and one brown.

LYMAN
(Beat)
Not me.

GERI
How much do you remember?

LYMAN
Not a lot. Too much. Not everything.

GERI
A young woman named Lily?

LYMAN
I didn't mess with any of the locals much. You couldn't
trust them.

GERI
I wonder why.

LYMAN
I didn't care.

GERI
Let me see your ID.

LYMAN

Don't carry one.

GERI

Sure you do.

LYMAN

I'm not your dad, don't worry about it.

GERI

What's your name? Do you know?

LYMAN

What was his?

GERI

I told you. Ray Farrow.

LYMAN

Say it again.

GERI

Ray Farrow.

LYMAN

No.
      (Pause)

GERI

Did you know him?

LYMAN

I wouldn't remember. What division was he in?

GERI

Infantry.

29

LYMAN

I was a combat engineer.

GERI

What do they do?

LYMAN

Blow up bridges. I said I wanted engineering. They said, great, combat engineering. Blow up everything an engineer builds.

GERI

My dad wanted to be a builder. You were studying architecture.

LYMAN

No.

GERI

What then?

LYMAN

I don't know, kid.

GERI

Where was school?

LYMAN

I don't think about it.

GERI

Where are you from? Where did you grow up? What kind of car did you drive around the town square? Who were the girls who wouldn't let you in? You joined the army because they told you you could choose your own training.

LYMAN
(He looks at her a moment)
Some joker came to our school, said enlist for three
years, choose your AIT.

GERI

Where?
(Beat)
What rank were you?

LYMAN

E4. Special Engineer.

GERI

Where are you from?

LYMAN

It doesn't matter now. I don't remember.

GERI

Nobody knows much about you. Or any of you. Maybe
as long as you all don't murder them in their beds, they
just count their blessings. You see homeless people, but
you guys wandering around Arcata and Eureka are dif-
ferent, aren't you? "Eureka." Wow, is that ever wrong.
What's Greek for "I've lost it"?

I asked this reporter on the *Arcata Union* how many
guys from Nam have drifted up here over the years,
hiding out behind the Redwood Curtain. They don't
even have a good estimate. Somewhere between three
and maybe eight thousand. A lot of latitude there.

All of you just move, float through town like specters.
All you ghosts. Wandering around the streets, working
odd jobs once a month, half high half the time, eating
out of garbage pails and what you can hunt. Probably
good hunters. Maybe you have a shack out here. Just a
piece of tin to keep the rain off you and your dog. You

wouldn't be cold with all those clothes. One of the guys I asked why have so many of you come here said it's a lot like Vietnam: quiet, beautiful, damp, the smell. Actually, a lot of them have told me that. I've been looking for you for a long time.

(He stands and a spell seems to be broken)

LYMAN

Sorry. Grew up in a city, no small town. No town square. Go on, now. Tell you something. Arcata's straight that way.

(He points down left)

Just take off, okay? Go on. Keep walking against the sun.

GERI

The sun that I caused to shine.

LYMAN

The fog burns off about this time every day.

GERI

Arcata's that way? You'd really say that? Boy. Just walk till I find it, huh? What if I really didn't know? I'd trust you and go that way. I really would get lost. What? Would that make your day or something? Knowing that I was wandering around lost at night? You and your dog could giggle over that, I guess.

LYMAN

You leave, I'll never think another thing about it. I'll forget I ever saw you in ten minutes. Guaranteed.

GERI

That's just the way you are, huh? Do you care that little about people, or do you just not retain things?

LYMAN

Fine. Whatever. It's the way you said. Down there. Just go on.

GERI

I mean, I don't know. Maybe you were shell-shocked or something. It clearly affected your mind somehow. I mean, you're not what anyone would call remotely normal.

LYMAN

Yeah? What's normal?

GERI

No no no no, sorry. Normal, whatever it is, is something far less of a sociopath. I mean, forgive me if that's a surprise to you.

LYMAN
(More to himself, but aloud)
First it's too damn cold, then it's too damn close. Fry your ass, boil, or something. Hot as hell in here and still wet.
(He takes off one sweater, then the other. He has on a T-shirt and a short-sleeved shirt that expose his white biceps with a tattoo of an eagle)

GERI

Oh, my God. Oh, my God. Oh, lord.

LYMAN

What? What now? Just go on.

GERI

Where did you get that tattoo? You have an eagle— who are you? You tell me your name. Right now.

> *(She looks dizzy, she holds her head, trying to maintain her balance)*

Oh, God. Oh, lord. Oh, lord.

> *She staggers a step, trying to straighten up, and faints dead away on the forest floor.*
>
> *The man looks at her. It is very still. He picks up her wallet and looks through it. He takes a picture out, pulling it from the sleeve, looking on the back for an inscription.*
>
> *An eagle cries out. The man looks up against the sun, shading his eyes.*
>
> *The lights fade to black.*

SCENE 2

The stage is black except for the headlights of a Mercedes pointing directly at the audience, the beams angled below eye level. In the spill of the dash light is GENEVA SIMONSON, a woman in her forties, who is driving. GERI is in the passenger seat, wearing a man's winter jacket. She leans against the window, looking out into the dark. Most of the time GENEVA manages to conceal her deep concern for GERI's well-being.

GENEVA

You say you're fine, so I'll believe you're fine, but you don't look fine at all. Zip that up, love. I'm surprised you're not frozen. This isn't La Jolla.
    (GERI zips up the jacket)
You were in the woods. And some man was in the woods. And you fainted. Did he jump out from behind a tree and go "Boo!"? I'm trying to construct a plausible scenario here.
    (Beat)
I hope to hell this wasn't another one of your father candidates. You know how I feel about that.
    (Nothing. More to herself than to GERI)
Nothing's more exasperating than a seventeen-year-old genius who thinks she can take care of herself. Your mother would literally kill me. She'd have me grilled and served on toast at one of her luncheons. And I'd deserve it. Alone. In the woods. At night. Accosted by a man.

I wasn't accosted, Aunt Geneva. I'm fine.

GENEVA
(A pause. She sighs)
You never hear about night vapors anymore, but I'm
sure that's what this is. The fog comes in across low tide
and picks up that really pleasant smell of beached sea-
weed. Or an inland wind brings over the aroma of the
pulp mills, and all the various chemicals involved in
that fragrant enterprise. Last August we had seven days
running where the temperature never got above 51 de-
grees. Two evenings in a row it was 36. And this is
August. Of course, it never quite manages to freeze
much. We did have snow last February. Almost half an
inch. They closed all the schools in a panic. Just as well,
the local drivers were at a total loss. Fender-bender
heaven. Answer to a body shop's prayers.
(Beat)
I'm not fooling myself. I'm just trying to hate Arcata so
I won't miss it.

GERI
You know you're never going to leave here.

GENEVA
I don't suppose you struck out this morning with the
intention of hiking all the way to some tourist trap
T-shirt emporium in the middle of the forest.
(Beat)
If you'd been—what time was it?—another fifteen min-
utes, those people would have closed and gone home.
Just be thankful they had a phone, not all of them do.

GERI
I'm sorry if I made you worry.

36

Kimiko Cazanov (left) as Geri with David Morse as Lyman. Set design by John Lee Beatty.

Photos of the 1992 Seattle Repertory Theatre/Circle Repertory Company presentation by Chris Bennion

David Morse (left) with Kimiko Cazanov.

Kimiko Cazanov (standing) with David Morse.

Debra Monk (left) as Geneva with Kimiko Cazanov.

GENEVA
(A beat)
Actually, we never thought a thing about it. We thought
you were at the movies. They don't get out for another
hour. Barney left just before you called. Some last-ditch
effort with the lawyers. Alas. Would that he were shtup-
ping his secretary, it'd be less a waste of time, and God
knows she needs it. But it just isn't in his nature. He's
always put sex in the same general category as exercise.
Too little reward for such great effort.
(She glances at GERI again)
That was a joke.
(Beat)
I'm trying to remember this one's name. The lawyer.
He says we've already lost the company. It's refreshing
to hear a lawyer tell the truth. We tried everything legal
there was to try. The judges just struck us down. This
outfit's going to clear-cut every tree in sight, they're
going to come through here with buzz saws. I just feel
the trees screaming at me. Can't you use some of your
magic to save them?

GERI
If I could, I'd have stopped you from cutting them down
a long time ago. I don't know why you're so scared of
them. They're trees, they won't bite you.

GENEVA
They could fall on me. I felt perfectly safe in the woods
when I knew for sure they were mine.

GERI
It's not your fault if you lose them.

GENEVA

I know that, but do they. Dad taught Laird and me how to drive down here on this road before it was paved. In a '52 Packard. It was an old car, you understand.

(She looks at GERI, who doesn't respond, and de-liberately changes the subject)

I think I'm going to be after a spot of tea. How does that strike you?

GERI

In bed maybe.

GENEVA

Are you being glum and sulky, or are you really not feeling well? I don't want you to get sick your last day here.

GERI

No, I'm just angry. Disappointed in myself.

GENEVA

Well, I'm almost never what I hope I'll be.

GERI

My shoulder hurts. I think I fell on it funny.

GENEVA

(Not a criticism, almost a complaint)

Nobody faints anymore. I don't think I ever have. I passed out cold once in the back seat of a car, but I was drunk. Four men in the car and not one of them took advantage of me. I wasn't always this beautiful. What's the sensation?

GERI

It was sort of like spacing. I tried to sit down so I wouldn't fall, but I don't think I made it.

GENEVA

Are you hungry?

    (GERI shakes her head)

Take a hot bath and I'll have Matilda bring your tea up to your room.

    (Pause. Then she sings lightly to herself)

"Matilda. Matilda. Matilda. She take me money and run Venezuela. Everybody . . ." I can never say her name without thinking of that.

GERI

She wouldn't dare.

GENEVA

Oh, if she could think of a way . . . Why didn't you buy a sweatshirt in that place? You could keep warm, at least.

GERI

The bastard stole my wallet.

GENEVA

Geri. Before you do anything, call your mother and tell her to call the credit-card people.

GERI

Julia would love that.

GENEVA

I'm who she'll blame. On second thought, call your mother's secretary. Her purpose in life seems to be lying to get you out of trouble, anyway.

GERI

Aunt Geneva, think. He couldn't possibly use them.

He could sell them, or throw them away and someone else could find them.

(They reach their destination. GENEVA sighs and closes her eyes a moment. She reaches to turn off the car lights; they dim as GERI is getting out of the car. We hear the car doors slam in the darkness. They speak over the dark a moment)

Tell Matilda to run your bath and I'll start the tea. And don't get exposure or something. I don't know how to treat it.

GERI

No, I'm fine now.

(A piano is heard playing the last movement of the Waldstein Sonata as the lights come up the following morning on the music room of a large and very fine Victorian house. GENEVA is listening to the tape of a recital. GERI enters as the movement ends)

What are you doing in here?

GENEVA

Don't turn it off, this is the best part.

GERI

Thanks.

(There is a burst of applause and cheering on the stereo. GERI turns it off in the middle)

GENEVA

It gives me goose bumps every time I hear it. That was San Diego.

GERI

I dropped the F natural at the end of the last run.

GENEVA

What's that note?

GERI

There are a lot of them.

GENEVA

The one you keep repeating. Bong, bong. You know
what I mean. I become so sensitized to that note I can
pick it out in a whole run. Which is what Beethoven
intended, I'm sure. Especially the way you bang on it.
Where is it? Go play it.

GERI

No, Aunt Geneva.

GENEVA

Just that one note.
> (*Rather than argue,* GERI *goes to the piano and
> hits the G twice.* GENEVA *groans in ecstasy*)

GERI

Why anyone would want to be involved, even periph-
erally, with music is beyond me. Nobody *ever* listens.
We go to the opera, everyone, I mean *everyone*, is asleep.
Music is Ovaltine to them. Mother had all these intel-
lectual types over, all they talked about all weekend was
this concert. Zubin Mehta was guest conductor on *Live
from London* or something, they all know him, of course.
They go in the TV room, they turn on the TV, they start
with the "He's let his hair grow, he looks very distin-
guished, I love his tails . . ." and the architectural detail
of Albert Hall, which they didn't like and you couldn't
see anyway, and all the music they've heard there, and
how foul the food was at the "interval," and all the
music they've heard all over Europe and the food they

had *there*, and finally just the *food* they've had. They didn't hear a note of music.

GENEVA

You should have taped it.

GERI

The point was to hear it live from London. Also, I don't know how to work the VCR. The one time I got it to tape anything, I set it to record *Cheers*, I came home, I'd taped an entire Yankee–Oakland game. The As literally cleaned New York's clock. Also, the program was "Mostly Mahler," which is not my idea of a fun evening.

GENEVA

You're sounding bitter.

GERI

You're darned right I'm bitter. I practice like a dog for twelve years, get exercised to tears over some nuance of theory for godsake over something nobody even hears. It's a rip-off. You know the average number of playing times for a CD? You don't, I read it last week —even pop records, the average number of times a record is played is one time and a quarter. And they want me to spend a week in some studio going over and over the *Goldberg Variations* like we need another recording of that? Forget it.

GENEVA
(After a moment she lets that pass)
Is that a good show, *Cheers*?

GERI

I love it, but I intend to marry Ted Danson. Do they really serve food during intermission at Albert Hall?

42

GENEVA

I imagine.

GERI

That is just so—typical. It's all Julia's friends talk about. During breakfast they talk about lunch; during lunch they start planning dinner. She had some winner of the National Book Award and this critic and a physicist and this Genius Painter and God knows how many really good musicians you might actually learn something from, sitting around the room arguing, and I mean almost to blows, over the best recipe for kreplach.

GENEVA

Which Mahler?

GERI

The Seventh. In E Minor, which is like insult to injury.

GENEVA

Is that why you're not practicing so much lately?

GERI

I'm not practicing at all. Ever again.

GENEVA

I can remember when you'd done a whole hour of scales by this time.

GERI

I thought I'd spare you.

GENEVA

You've always said you like this piano. Maybe we should trade. This one really belonged to your dad. Nobody ever plays it except you. If you like it better.

43

GERI

I don't want any of them. Leave it here.

GENEVA

My best memory of this room is bringing my breakfast in here at the crack of dawn and watching you play. Your dad conducting with a cigarette, counting out the time like a metronome.

GERI

A cigarette in one hand and a bottle of white wine in the other. You had to get to Laird before noon; his day was usually over about lunchtime.

GENEVA

I like scales and exercises. I always have. The sound of industry maybe.

GERI

(She glares mildly at GENEVA)
You're really pushing it. Do you love the sawmill?

GENEVA

I loved the smell, not the noise.

GERI

If you really don't know I quit, I mean totally quit, then you're the only person in the nation that doesn't know, because Julia's been like broadcasting it. She doesn't really care but it's thrilling conversation. I'm going to Paris and—I don't know, study cooking. Learn to do something people understand.

GENEVA

(She lets that pass)
You seem to have recovered from your ordeal in the forest.

It was my own fault. I have to get ready, some of the guys are going down to the river.

GENEVA

Who was this "he" who caused you to faint? You were following another one of your Gray Eminences, weren't you?
  (GERI *doesn't answer*)
Geri, we cannot have you harassing those men.

GERI

I don't.

GENEVA

You do, too, Geri, and it's cruel. Also, you can't know when one will be dangerous. Most of them are army men, you realize. Trained at great expense to be homicidal.
  (*Beat*)
Who were you this time? Of them all, I think I like the anarchist exchange student from the Philippines trying to recruit a network of underground spies.

GERI

Moles.

GENEVA

How you get them to talk to you, I'll never know. They won't to most people.

GERI

Most people don't want them to.

GENEVA

No, darling, that doesn't wash. I've said good morning several times and they've never even looked at me. You

draw them out, get them talking about their lives, their
war experiences that they clearly don't want to remember or they wouldn't be here. "Do you know my real
father, his name is Ray Farrow, he has eyes like mine
that don't match." I can't leave you alone for five minutes, you've got another one cornered. It isn't fair to
Julia, it's an insult to Laird. I know you don't see it that
way, but your mother would shit a brick.

GERI

She isn't my mother.

GENEVA

Geri, you just exasperate the hell out of me. If Julia isn't
your mother, Laird wasn't your father, I'm not your
aunt, and you're a penniless little waif in some Dick-
ensian orphanage. You have to take her as she comes
and she'd shit a brick.

GERI

I know. But she's so uptight she shits bricks at the least
breach of etiquette. You could build a small village with
the bricks Mother's shat. It was bad enough when Laird
was alive, pretending she didn't see he was like falling
down drunk all the time, and I mean that took effort.
But there's nothing of her in me at all. She's a fabulous
mother—

GENEVA

—She lets you do anything you damn well please.

GERI

But it's not all that weird to wonder who I am, is it?

GENEVA

You're very lucky. Most kids have no proof when they
feel there must have been some tragic mix-up in the

46

hospital and these people they live with couldn't possibly be their real parents. You at least *know* you were adopted. That should be some consolation.

GERI

It isn't.

GENEVA

I don't know. I've watched you almost month by month develop into such a fine, talented young woman—you and Laird working so hard. You couldn't have been five, he knew already you were going to be better than he'd ever dreamed of being. By the time you were seven, any fool could see it. I just feel I know you so well, I can't understand why you don't know yourself. You're just deliberately moving away from us. I expect any day now you'll start spouting Vietnamese and wearing a kimono.

GERI

They don't wear kimonos. I know too much already and I don't know how I know it. A father over there literally *owns* his family. He could sell them if he wanted to.

GENEVA

I wonder how much we could get for you.

GERI

The whole family answers to the father; then the father answers only to the mandarin; and the mandarin answers only to the emperor. I think I'm mandarin.

GENEVA

Go for emperor.

GERI

It's scary. It just slams into my head. I just suddenly know, or I hear, or something: "Good conduct is learn-

47

ing to do exactly what your father did. Every movement a perfect repetition of his. Answer to your father before you."

(Beat)

And I think, you know (*a*) That's a crock. And (*b*) And we wonder why all the Vietnam kids are looking for their fathers? Wake up and learn something, God! And (*c*) Where the hell did that *come* from? And I appreciate that information a hell of a lot, but I have no idea what my father *did* before me, so like bugger off, okay?

(Less agitated)

My ancestors' ashes have been scattered in a field over there, for a hundred generations. Three thousand years. So they're literally, physically nourishing their descendants. Or this voice says, "If you do everything correctly," which is exactly as it's always been done, I suppose, to the last detail, "then you'll be content. Fields will prosper, the weather will be fair, and calm will prevail."

GENEVA

I don't understand those rice cultures.

GERI

Obviously not. You're selling everything your ancestors have done down the toilet.

GENEVA

The hell I am. We've spent a fortune fighting those SOBs.

GERI

Oh, I don't care. Do what you have to do. Who am *I*? How do I do what my father has done before me? What? Should I go to war and come back and drink myself under the table every night like Laird? Or, being a woman, I'll go around like Julia dragging my sable from

48

one board meeting to another, dropping a hundred thousand dollars on every charity that licks my ass.

GENEVA

Geri, please! Every charity that *kisses* your ass, not licks your ass.

GERI
(Pause)
I like the sound, though. "And calm will prevail."

GENEVA
(Beat)
It has a definite ring.

GERI

I was talking to the man Buzz Warren ran over in the alley.

GENEVA

Oh, good lord. John Doe? No wonder you fainted.

GERI

He has a name.

GENEVA

Well, if he does, he doesn't know it. Elaine said he didn't even know his own name. Mumbled and jumbled and left before they'd set his foot properly.

GERI

He talks fine. He's just very private.

GENEVA

That's clear, I think.

GERI

And a thief, but I don't blame him.

GENEVA

How much money did you give him?

GERI

Give? I didn't give—

GENEVA

What were you carrying?

GERI

Six hundred.

GENEVA

Oh, good lord. If you weren't going home tomorrow, I think I'd send you back anyway.

GERI

I wasn't planning on fainting. It must have been the sun. I was so eager to flaunt my powers I banished every trace of cloud cover. It got hot as the devil in there.

GENEVA

That was you? I had to turn on the air conditioner. Julia is going to have to talk to you about managing your money.

GERI

I know from her example: Unless they name a building after you, never, under any circumstances, let go of a single nickel.

GENEVA

I don't know. For entertainment we used to go roller-skating. For mental stimulation we'd read a good book.

It was always a *good* book, we never said I'd like to curl up with just a book. He is absolutely the last one you talk to.

GERI
Okay.

GENEVA
I mean it. What's his name?

GERI
He didn't tell me. He blew up bridges. It destroyed his hearing, I think.

GENEVA
That'd be the least of his afflictions. They must have earplugs. Besides, they can't just stand there and watch it blow up.

GERI
He's growing pot out in your woods.

GENEVA
He didn't happen to give you any, for your trouble? Some very good ganja has come out of those woods. I've come across whole farms of it. I was walking along, carrying David, he couldn't have been more than two, and suddenly came out into this clearing with a little house and a very big man with an even bigger dog and a shotgun. I just said, "Oh, I'm terribly sorry, we were looking for the river," turned around and walked straight home, thank you. Expecting to be shot in the back of the head with every step. That's another reason I don't want you wandering around out there.

Also, they don't belong to us anymore. We don't belong there. God, it kills me to say that. I don't have a memory, there's not a single family story that isn't con-

51

nected to those trees. If I'm not a lumberjack, I don't know what the hell I am.

GERI

They're never going to finalize the sale.

GENEVA

Takeover! There was no damn sale, we weren't *for* sale!

GERI

Yeah, but you know lawyers, they'll drag it out for centuries.

GENEVA

All done. This morning. While you were getting your beauty sleep. We caved in. Or bit the bullet.

GERI

Oh, no.

GENEVA

Well, it was over.

GERI

I mean, Julia said not to bring it up because you couldn't possibly win, but I'm so used to you fighting them.

GENEVA

No more. And don't get used to things. We signed our names with a flourish on a hundred lines. I've never been so angry in my life. Or felt so impotent. Barney chain-smoking. He kept saying, I know you hate the smoke, but I can't not smoke right now. If he's buying something or selling something. He thinks he's let my family down. They let themselves down, going public in the first place. Who'd ever heard of a takeover back

52

then. Everybody said it'll still just be a little family concern.

Sure. Some bastard offers twice what the stock is going for, all your "buddies" on the board fall all over themselves to be first in line. You'd think they'd be terribly disappointed in themselves to discover they have their price. Hell, no. They're not lumbermen anymore, they're moguls.

GERI

You'll be pretty well compensated, though.

GENEVA

The point isn't the money. The point is some no-name gasket company from Pittsburgh and some CEO from Houston can take over a hundred-twenty-year-old family company and just trash it.

GERI

How much will you get, though?

GENEVA

Oh—it's been reported in every paper in the country. We have twenty percent of the holding; they're getting seven hundred million, fifty dollars a share.

GERI

A hundred forty million.

GENEVA

Hardly. Taxes, love. To death. Less than half that.

GERI

A lousy sixty million dollars.

What the hell are we going to do with money like that?
We're not your mother and her jet-set crowd.
(Beat)
And it isn't enough. I could say I cared for a hundred
thousand acres of redwood forest. The oldest living
thing. I was on a goddamned float in the parade when
I was ten, dressed like a shepherdess, with hundreds of
little knee-high trees around me. Shepherdess of the
Redwoods.
(GERI is smiling)
Well, damnit, I *felt* like the Shepherdess of the Redwoods. I don't expect a damn wood nymph to understand, but I did! We've cut them so conscientiously;
everyone in town thought we were too conservative.
Even the goddamned Sierra Club approved! We were
harvesting trees my great-great-grandfather planted.
These guys have borrowed all that money. You can't
manage a forest from debt. They're just going to mow
them down. Environmentalists are gonna have a field
day, honey. The fertilizer is gonna hit the ol' fan.

GERI

Maybe the new manager won't be that bad.

GENEVA

The man is from Texas, there's not a tree in the state.
Prosperity for ten years, then this burg will be a ghost
town.

GERI

You knew it was coming, though; you always said you
couldn't win. You haven't set foot in the forest since
that company made their first bid.

Well, not my problem anymore. Not Barney's problem. To hell with all of them. But I'm angry. It's very easy to be a success in this world, Geri. All you have to do is change your goals.

GERI

Maybe it was just time to retire.

GENEVA

Geri, nobody likes it when you take this devil's advocate position. It's not about the money. If I wanted to be rich I could be rich. You get a job at a security-exchange house, practice insider trading, make eight hundred million dollars, get caught, get convicted, pay five hundred million in fines and taxes, go to jail for five years, get out in two. I know very few men of thirty who wouldn't spend two years in jail for three hundred million dollars.

(Beat)

And I don't like the way you throw around phrases like "It's time for you to retire." These bastards are cutting me off at the roots. Forcing me out of my own damn house.

GERI

You wouldn't leave Arcata.

GENEVA

Go look out on the front lawn. The sign went up this morning.

GERI

No.

55

GENEVA

Damned if I'm going to be the brunt of all the local indignation when the boom busts. The real-estate Dough Boy was literally salivating. He said, We'll just keep this listing between ourselves. I said, No way! I want the whole State of California to know I'm out of here. Put up a sign with the finger on it.

GERI

You can't leave here.

GENEVA

You just watch me.

GERI

I spend the whole year waiting to come up here.

GENEVA

You'll like Key Biscayne just as well.

GERI

I hate Key Biscayne. You hate Key Biscayne.

GENEVA

Well, tough. Barney loves it. He thinks he's a deep-sea fisherman. He said, If you really want it, we can pick up some land south of Eureka, but no more. No more logging. It really is going to be nice to sit on my butt and not panic every time I smell smoke; looking at the sky to see if it's ever going to rain. Wondering if it would look too showy for this town if I got a new car or a chauffeur. We'll be somewhere where everyone has money and nobody has an attack if you spend it. And I don't care how that sounds. We've done a good job.

GERI

If I can't come here—I'll never find him. This one is
really not like the others.

GENEVA
(Deliberately changing the subject)
You think you could manage breakfast before you hit
the river?

GERI
No.

GENEVA

Geri, no! You are not to go looking for that man. Or
any of them. They don't want it, it isn't fair to them.
You're just setting yourself up for another disappoint-
ment.

GERI

How do you know he doesn't want it?

GENEVA

Well, does he present an invitation to society, in your
view?

GERI

Who knows? Maybe he just doesn't know—

GENEVA

No, darling, thank you, but my own brother came back
from that war totally wacko. Laird never drank before.
If you're going to visit us, we have to be responsible for
you. You're not just any old curious tomboy; you're
rather special, you know. You're one of the best young
pianists this country has ever produced.

57

GERI

My decision on that is absolutely final.

GENEVA

If you have a talent like that, you have no choice but to practice it.

GERI

That's the Protestant Ethic; it has nothing to do with Asians.

GENEVA

Oh, you drive me crazy sometimes.

GERI

And I'd as soon give up the magic while I'm at it. Where has it got me except for being the adopted daughter of a wealthy family that lets me do anything I please.

GENEVA

It isn't funny. Julia really would just let you throw it all away. I could just shake her. I can't wait to tell her you've decided to be a cook.

GERI

As long as it doesn't inconvenience her summers in Italy. My schedule was getting a little heavy for her, anyway.

GENEVA

She says you haven't practiced in two months. You haven't touched the piano since you've been here. I've listened every morning, waiting to hear you play. Did you cancel your recital in Chicago?

GERI

Yes. And the recording session. All of it. I'm not joking.

GENEVA

Are you tired?

GERI

I'm not tired, damnit, I've just had it. And I don't think it's at all unusual or sick or egocentric to want to be a normal human being or to be liked or appreciated in something.

GENEVA

You're appreciated. Enormously.

GERI

I'm not appreciated, I'm "special." Every time I walk out onstage. "Oh, isn't she tiny, isn't she just adorable. She's a Vietnam War bastard, you know. She has no idea who her mother and father are. Aren't we lucky one of them turned out to be special." Sony Classical wanted to call my album "America's Children"!

And I don't see why having a talent or a gift, even if it's for just sticking at something and sitting on my rear end and practicing, which is all I have, anyway—I have a tolerance for repeating scales and exercises ad nauseam; apparently I enjoy my fingers swelling up and having my nails bleed and walking around with Band-Aids on all my fingers—and I don't know why someone with whatever that is, that gift or curse or liability or handicap (it's like you can only be given something, even of whatever questionable value, if you're simultaneously eviscerated of everything anyone holds as worthy or admirable or real or worthwhile), I don't know why someone like that has to be treated like a freak of nature, like they have seven arms like Shiva or however many he has, and tiptoed around like they're sick or maimed or consumptive or an invalid or special in some way. I don't want to be special.

(Pause)

59

GENEVA

You're special, Geri.
(Pause)

GERI

I know I am.
(She walks out of the room)

GENEVA

Honey.

GERI

(Off)
I'm going down to the river.

GENEVA

Let me drive you.

GERI

(Off)
No.
(We hear the front door slam. After a moment, behind GENEVA, LYMAN appears in the open doorway. She hears him and turns, seeing him)

GENEVA

(Starting)
Oh. Dear God in heaven.

LYMAN

You Mrs. Smith?

GENEVA

(After she collects herself)
I have the feeling that my niece was possibly rude to you yesterday and owes you an apology. She isn't in just now, but maybe you'll accept mine.

(Beat)

And I believe that you inadvertently took something that belongs to her.

LYMAN

Your husband Dr. Smith?

GENEVA

No.

LYMAN

He teach arithmetic at the school?

GENEVA

My husband? My husband drives down to the mill once a month and walks through with a great grin on his face, saying, "Lookin' good, boys, lookin' good, boys," gets back in his car, drives home, comes in the house and says, "It's lookin' good, Genny."
(Beat)
He also pays the bills and signs the paychecks.
(Beat)
I was just getting ready to go out. So I'm afraid I'm going to have to ask you to leave.

LYMAN

(Flashing GERI's photograph from her wallet)
You know this girl?

GENEVA

That's my niece.
(She reaches for the wallet; he doesn't offer it)

LYMAN

What's her name?

GENEVA

Geri Riordan. It's probably in there.

LYMAN

Her name's not Geraldine Lon?

GENEVA

She has a phony driver's license with the name Geraldine Lon on it that says she's of age. I'm not supposed to know that. She had them put down Lon as a joke.
　　(Beat)
I guess you had to be there. We call her Geri. But her name is Riordan, not Lon.

LYMAN

　　(He flashes another picture)
That her mother?

GENEVA

Geri, what the hell have you been doing. That's a photograph of some Chinese film star, Geri doesn't even know her name. No, that's not Geri's mother. She has a rather eccentric sense of humor.

LYMAN

　　(Holds up another photo)
That her foster dad?

GENEVA

Yes.

LYMAN

He drink himself to death?

GENEVA

Laird was my brother. He came home from the war very troubled. You might understand that. Or not.

LYMAN

She live here?

GENEVA

No. Now, if you'll—

LYMAN

She said she was staying with Dr. Smith.

GENEVA

I don't know any damn Dr. Smith. I don't know Mrs.
Smith. Off the top of my head, I don't think I've ever
known a Smith in my life.

LYMAN
(He hands her the wallet)
Count the money.

GENEVA

It's fine, I'm sure.

LYMAN

Count the money!

GENEVA

I'm sure it's—well, why not? One, two, three, four. Six
hundred dollars. It's remarkable to get it back with that
much cash.

LYMAN

Where would I break a fifty-dollar bill?

GENEVA

Mr. Doe. Let's just not thrash around that bush, okay?
There are ten bars in Arcata that would happily serve
a baboon with the price of a drink. If you're hinting for

a reward, it's the most ludicrous suggestion I've ever heard.

You let her follow people around town? Let her walk around town with money like that?

LYMAN
GENEVA
Thank you for returning this. She'll be very glad to have it back. Now, if you'll—

LYMAN
She ever tell the truth?
(GENEVA is preparing to close the door in his face)
She telling the truth when she said her dad was to Vietnam?
(She is stopped dead a moment. She looks over his shoulder to the yard)

GENEVA
(Not a reprimand)
Is that your dog out in my dahlias?
(Beat)
What's her name?

LYMAN
I call her Bitch.

GENEVA
I have a friend who would say, "Droll." I'm sure it's all in the tone of the voice. Mr. . . . . I don't know what my niece has been telling you. She's visiting here for the month. She does every June, since she was twelve. She goes home tomorrow. She has a habit of talking to strangers.

LYMAN

She told me she'd never seen the trees before.

GENEVA

Well, as I said, she's here every summer.

LYMAN

She said her dad's name was Ray Farrow.

GENEVA

She's— No. No, I'm not going to go into this with you.
I'll apologize for any inconvenience Geri's caused you.
I'm . . . sorry about your hearing, you cope very well.

LYMAN

I hear okay.

GENEVA

I understood you blew up bridges in the war.

LYMAN

Yeah.

GENEVA

And it impaired your hearing.

LYMAN

You wear plugs.

GENEVA

I see.
        (He hands her a set of dog tags)

LYMAN

I put these on the dog, I don't wear them anymore.

65

GENEVA

You keep your dog tags on your dog. That's very . . .
(She reads the tag)
This is you? "Lyman Fellers"?
(He gives no indication. After a moment)
Come in, have a seat.

LYMAN

I'm fine.
(He remains standing in the doorway. GENEVA walks around the room a moment, landing at the bar)

GENEVA

You didn't tell Geri your name.

LYMAN

That doesn't matter.

GENEVA

It'll matter a hell of a lot to her. What did she tell you?

LYMAN

She's looking for her dad.

GENEVA

Yes, well, all of them are, aren't they? Half the people in America are looking for their fathers. You see it on television all the time. Hopelessly arrogant young men and women claiming their right to know their biological parents at whatever cost to everyone else.

Julia always said you'd turn up one day. They spotted you in Hopland a few years back, gave us a general description of who you were, she nearly died.

That's the only reason Geri comes here. She's been systematically interviewing all of you . . .
(She gropes for a word to call them, then goes on)

66

in the whole Great Northwest Territory. Every June since she was twelve.

(*Pause. She looks at the dog tags, rubbing one between her thumb and finger*)

I'm not ready for this. You should know that Geri's mother gave her up for adoption the moment she set foot in this country. Geri was less than a month old. The only information we've had about you is what she told us: the father was a serviceman named Farrow. With one brown—

(*Looking him directly in the face, she breaks off*)

Oh, dear God—well, I knew that, didn't I?

(*She musters on through*)

Who had one blue eye and one brown and a tattoo of an eagle on his arm. I'll take that on faith. She gave her name as Lily Lon. Subsequent investigations proved that information erron—why am I talking like that?

The name Lily Lon was a phony. I always thought your description was so farfetched that you were a figment, too. My brother Laird just laughed. Geri's bought it, of course. I probably would, too, if that was the only thing I had.

(*Beat*)

Geri has been well loved and cared for. As it happens, she's developed into one of the most promising pianists to come down the pike in a hell of a long time. She had her first recital five years ago. She's been all over the country. And England and France. Japan. She just completed a tour with the St. Louis Symphony. She's exhausted; she's trying to do too much. She finished school, she was going to go to Juilliard next year on a full scholarship. Right now she's off music; I don't know what the hell she wants.

LYMAN

She's not looking at schools?

67

What? No. The only thing she cares about is "finding herself." I thought we finished with that in the sixties. This is tragic. Excuse me, but your timing couldn't be worse.

LYMAN

She knows plants?

GENEVA

What?

LYMAN

She studies plants?

GENEVA

No. I don't know what she's told you. You shouldn't—

LYMAN

She said her dad grew up in a small town.

GENEVA

We weren't told that. She guesses as much as she knows.

LYMAN

She said her mother owned a flower shop in Nam.

GENEVA

Her mother was a child, fourteen or fifteen as I'm sure you well know. She barely knew English. My brother and his wife gave the girl twenty-five thousand dollars for Geri. The adoption was totally legal but definitely not through the usual channels; if you want to make something of that. The usual channels are too slow for Julia.

68

LYMAN

Shrewd cookie. Drives a stiff bargain.

GENEVA

Whatever. I imagine if the father showed up and agreed
to waive all claims, and not attempt to see Geri again,
he could expect to get at least that much.
(Beat)
Probably a good deal more. I'll give you a number you
can call.

LYMAN

He built stuff?

GENEVA

I'm sorry?

LYMAN

Geri said her dad was studying to be a builder.

GENEVA

We don't know that. We've never known anything about
what her natural father did.
(Pause)

LYMAN

I wanted to build things.

GENEVA

Oh, my God.
*(She is having a mild but sincere attack of
empathy)*
Mr. Fellers, I don't know what to say. I'll just kill her,
I really will. I'll just take a ball bat—

(Beat)
What do you want? Just tell me what it is you want.

LYMAN
You tell your niece not to talk to strangers.
He turns and leaves.
The lights fade to black.

SCENE 3

A coffeehouse in Arcata. GERI sits at a table with
a cup of coffee, studying a map. After a moment,
GENEVA enters. She walks to the table and drops
GERI's wallet on it.

GENEVA

Your putative father and Bitch dropped by the house.
Get your stuff together and let's get out of here. This
coffeehouse refuses to serve me. I sat here once for half
an hour, nobody gave me the time of day.

GERI

They don't have table service, you have to go to the
counter.

GENEVA

I'm too old to live in a college town.

GERI

What did he tell you?

GENEVA

He showed me his dog tags, probably the only identification he has. Right now, you've got that man so confused I don't think he knows if he's your father or not.

GERI

I think he is. What's his name?

71

GENEVA

If I told you it was nothing like Ray, would you still try to see him?

GERI

Are you crazy?

GENEVA

That's what I thought.
(She sits)
He was obviously skulking around the house, waiting for you to leave. He showed up the moment you left. It was all I could do not to hit the panic button and call Julia. It took me a full hour to get myself together enough to try to find him.

GERI

Why?

GENEVA

You're not going to talk to that man again unless I'm there. I've driven up and down every street and alley in Arcata. Halfway to Ferndale, up 101 damn near to Larrupin'. I've put ninety miles on the car. I saw one of your swimming buddies in town.

GERI

I didn't go swimming.

GENEVA

I realize that. I asked the woman at the shelter if she'd seen John Doe, she said, "Oh, Geri was just asking about him." You didn't find him?

GERI

No. I think he's gone back to the woods.

GENEVA

Oh, God. I can't do it. I can't go back in there.
   (Beat)
His name is Lyman Fellers.

GERI

Lyman Fellers? I don't care. He has an eagle tattooed
on his arm.

GENEVA

Ten thousand soldiers must have that tattoo. You told
him about that, too?

GERI

No.

GENEVA

Well, it doesn't matter. I did. What is that, a map?

GERI

   (Showing GENEVA *the map)*
I think we were here. The closest place you could drive
to is over here.

GENEVA

That's the other side of the fern valley. I can hardly
tramp through the woods dressed like this.

GERI

You know the way better than I do. It's not that far. If
you go by the house you'll want to change clothes, then
you'll want to leave a note for Barney. It'll be dark. I'm
going. You can take me or not.

GENEVA

Geri, I'm exhausted. Is there sugar in that?

73

No.

> (GENEVA *puts sugar in the coffee, stirs it, and drinks it down*)

GENEVA

Child, child, child. Why you want your father to be someone like that is . . .

GERI

I don't want it or not, I just think it's true. Don't you feel it? That kind of completely inhuman, asocial behavior. Wandering around by myself. Shut up in a two-by-four rehearsal room eight hours a day. Having so few friends. Not believing anything anyone says to me.

GENEVA

Well, whose fault is that?

GERI

Maybe it's his.

GENEVA

And no, I don't feel it. You're an artist. Artists are crazy.

GERI

No more.

GENEVA

Geri, he's not well. He's been—he's a—I'm trying to think of a way to talk about the man without sounding prejudicial or maudlin or—well, I can't.

But that's a fine reason to want to know your parents: having someone to blame your idiosyncrasies on. You actually followed him through the woods?

GERI

I thought maybe he'd, I don't know, *sing* to himself, or whistle or something.

GENEVA

Oh, God. If this doesn't kill me, Julia will kill me. Did he? Whistle?

GERI

He knew I was following him.

GENEVA

I whistle. I've even been known to sing to myself. Julia played the piano. David thinks he can play the guitar—

GERI

—Julia's never touched that piano in her life. It was Laird's piano.

GENEVA

You were brought up in a household that appreciates music. Some things are *learned*, Geri.

GERI

Some things are not.
        (They stand. The table goes away. The lights come up on the woods; they walk into it, calling)
Hello! Hello! What'd he tell you his name was?

GENEVA

Lyman Fellers.

GERI

        (Calling)
Mr. Fellers! Mr. Fellers!

(She waits, listening)
Well, there's no sign of him at all.

GENEVA

This is killing me. It's just ripping my heart out.

GERI

I wasn't thinking, did we walk too fast?

GENEVA

You unfeeling little wretch. I'm as strong as a horse. Most of my friends say I look almost exactly like a horse. I don't care if you *don't* ever get winded, I can run you around these woods ten times.

They're not *mine* anymore, Geri. I'm seeing them, I'm walking through them, it's just ripping my heart out.

GERI

I know. But they didn't fall on you.

GENEVA

Oh, God. Is this where he was?

GERI

Yes.
(She is looking through the wallet)
He's been through every thing in here. All the pictures have been taken out and put back the opposite of the way they were. Maybe he's dyslexic on top of everything else. He's even been at the secret compartment.

GENEVA

What have you got in there?

GERI

Nothing. Every wallet has one, what's the point? My library card, the note from Tom.

GENEVA

What did he mean, "Dear Geri, Thanks for the heart attack. Love, Tom"?

GERI

I knew you did that, that just burns me up. Tom told me he didn't want to take Phys. Ed. I told him to go to the nurse and complain of a pain in his chest and she'd give him an EKG that said he had a fluttery heart and they'd excuse him from Phys. Ed.

GENEVA

Does he have a fluttery heart?

GERI

Of course not. I only gave him a fluttery heart while he was having the EKG.

GENEVA

Does any of that sorcery—well, not that—genie-ness ever get you anything worthwhile? Like learning a new mazurka or doubling your considerable fortune?

GERI

No. I think it's supposed to guide me; it's not doing a very good job.
> *(There is the sound of a twig breaking off in the woods. They freeze, listening. GERI calls lightly)*

I know you'll come out when you want to.

GENEVA

God, this is a beautiful spot. Dad used to carry me
through here on his shoulders. I'm just being bom-
barded with memories of—are you doing some
    (Gestures)
fairy-dust number on me or something? I'm feeling very
weird here.

GERI

I have no idea what you're talking about.

GENEVA

You should think about what you're going to say if he
shows up. The man's obviously been mulling over every
stupid thing you told him. Dr. Smith? Geraldine Lon?
Your mother sold flowers?

GERI

She did.

GENEVA

How do you know she—well, I won't ask. You'll only
say "I never know."

GERI

I don't.
    (Calling)
Mr. Fellers!
    (To GENEVA*)*
What if he isn't? That'd be worse than if he were. He
said he never fraternized. That's hardly something you'd
forget. I mean, you'd expect the man to remember if
he'd got laid.

GENEVA

Geri.

GERI

And his name is wrong.

GENEVA

Lyman Fellers? Oh, we've known that name for years.

GERI

We have?

GENEVA

Your people, the agency, whatever they're called, who hunt down children's parents, must have told you about the man in Hopland.

GERI

It had to be Ray Farrow, how many people look like that? But he didn't have any identification.

GENEVA

Julia and Laird just saw that his name got lost in the report.

GERI

What was his name then?

GENEVA

The man in Hopland? Your buddy. Lyman Fellers.

GERI

Well, that's wrong. Unless I've been lied to all my life.

GENEVA

Wouldn't that be poetic justice. No, they've always told you what your natural mother said. That's the point.
        (She sits on a stump or rock, makes herself
        comfortable)

79

Have you met Suki Sato? Secretary of the Village Improvement Association of Key Biscayne.

GERI

No.

GENEVA

Wonderful Japanese lady. Used to answer the phone "Vera's Employment." We adored her. One Christmas—they have this Yuletide lobster pig-out dance. A kind of Tex-Mex luau. David and Sharon were supposed to go but they were having their biennial brabble. I was on the phone with Suki. I said I thought it was pretty useless to expect David and Sharon, or at least to expect them to come together. And she sighed and said, "Aw, Rubber Squirrel." We adored her. I had no idea what she was talking about half the time. Well, you know me, I never listen to anyone, really. I just said, Fine, whatever.

Naturally, I was driving. In the middle of the Richenbacher Causeway, I started laughing so hard I had to pull over or get us killed. Barney. I explained it to him. Maybe you had to be there. He still doesn't get it.

GERI

Get what?

GENEVA

They were having a "Rubber Squirrel," Geri.
        (Beat)
"Lover's quarrel."
        (Pause. GERI gives no indication of understanding)

GERI

It's an area of humor I've never really responded to.

80

GENEVA

I swear to God your brain has gone to pulp. You're as dumb as lumber sometimes. Geri. "Lover's quarrel," "Rubber Squirrel." "Lyman Fellers" . . . "Rymond Farrow"—

GERI

—Raymond Farrow. Oh, but that's really reaching.

GENEVA

Nevertheless, that's what Mr. Fellers has been thinking. I imagine he heard his name pronounced just that way over there. When Julia heard it, it scared her spitless.

GERI

I'd guess. What? Scandal, blackmail, bribery.

GENEVA

It isn't a joke. No, she was afraid of losing you. That's why she's so damned overprotective. You're the only thing she has she couldn't bear to lose.

GERI
(Unmoved)
That has to be underscored with like Mendelssohn or something.
(Beat)
Lyman Fellers. He really may be my father, then.

GENEVA

I got the impression he's not going to admit it. And if that's his game, fine. You're going to find out if he's willing to tell you anything about the circumstances of your birth, apologize for messing his mind up, and we're getting out of here.

GERI

If he's my father, I'm not going to just leave him here.

GENEVA

If that's what he wants, you certainly will.

GERI

It isn't what he wants.

GENEVA

You don't know that.

GERI

I do, too.

GENEVA

You do not.

GERI

I do, too.

GENEVA

Oh, lordy. Your mother will kill me. She'd have you as
far away from "Raymond Farrow" as she could get you.
Rome.
    (Beat)
God, the smell out here! They're going to cut this whole
place flat. You may as well know that I told him it'd
probably be worth a lot of money if he disappeared.

GERI

What?

GENEVA

Well, it will be.

82

GERI

Do you have any idea what this means to me?

GENEVA

I was thinking what it means to us.

GERI

What did he say?

GENEVA

I was so circumspect and he was so confused, I don't think he even knew I was trying to buy him off. Watch him come here now and say yes, I'm your father, what's it worth?

GERI

At least I'd know.

GENEVA

Oh, fine. And how are you going to follow in your father's footsteps in the time-honored tradition of the Vietnamese? Bang yourself over the head with a board and walk around La Jolla like a bag lady?
   (Beat)
You're already weird.
   (She looks down at GERI, who seems lost in thought, her energy gone)

GERI

He wanted to be an engineer.

GENEVA

I know, he told me. Oh, lordy. What in the deep rocky hell is life supposed to be about? If you want to be an engineer, you think you have to be an engineer, then be a damn engineer.
   (Beat)

83

You're so strong and you have such energy, and such superhuman talent, I forget how young you are, chicken. Why don't we go on home? Huh? It's going to start getting cold, then it'll be dark. Then it'll really get cold.
(*She is looking around her at the trees*)
God, it's so quiet here.

I don't think I can let them go, Geri. That stupid gasket company is going to need cash so badly . . . I think they'd jump at the chance to sell some of it off. I could buy back this section. Down to the fern valley.

GERI

"Shepherdess of the Redwoods"—?

GENEVA

—I knew I'd regret telling you that.

GERI

You don't have the sawmill anymore, you couldn't work it.

GENEVA

I'd have the trees.

GERI

Could you afford to just have them?

GENEVA

Well, I'm not saying I wouldn't keep something to live on.

GERI

Uncle Barney would hate it.

GENEVA

He really would. He loves Key Biscayne. He sees us retiring as the Old Man and the Sea and His Old Lady.

84

Never get married, Geri, your whole life is a compromise.

> (*A pause. A dog barks, not too far off.* GERI *and* GENEVA *look up.* LYMAN *is standing watching them. He walks toward them, looking at* GERI *all the while. After a moment he addresses* GERI)

LYMAN

I hunt. I fish sometimes. I don't eat garbage. There's a coffee-shop place called Wildflower, the lady leaves rolls out sometimes.

GENEVA

They use almost no butter in their cooking.

GERI

Aunt Geneva.

GENEVA

Well, I'm sorry. Barney and I eat there all the time.

LYMAN

I built a shelter place where I sleep 'cause of the rain. It's not bad.

GERI

Good.

LYMAN

I'm fine.

GERI

Good.

LYMAN

Were you really dead?

85

GERI

Yes.

LYMAN

You didn't see the White Light.

GERI

No.

LYMAN

What did you see?

GERI

Nothing.

LYMAN

You have a plastic hip?

GENEVA

Geri, what have you been telling him? She was on the operating table for seven hours.

GERI

I came close to having to have one. And a steel rod in my spine, too. They would have if it hadn't been for my heart. Really.

LYMAN

Yeah.

GERI

The doctor told me. You can ask him.

LYMAN

You been all over. You probably already seen a maze.

GERI

Hampton Court in Middlesex. It works, I tried it.

LYMAN

Your mother sell flowers in Saigon?

GENEVA

We don't know what she did or where she came from.

GERI

She did.

LYMAN

I grew up in Akron.

GENEVA

Where?

LYMAN

Akron. Ohio, ma'am. My dad had a garage I worked in. I enlisted senior year out of high school. I didn't have no girlfriends; they never said yes or no. Wasn't any square to drive around; we was all jet heads. Drag-raced. Muscle cars; ride around alone, act like fools. I had a Mustang. Boss 302. Za good car.

GERI

I'll bet you were good. That sounds patronizing. I don't mean it that way. I meant, I'll bet you were good.

LYMAN

I won some.

GENEVA

Mr. Fellers, Geri has something she'd like to say to you.
        (Pause. GERI studies him a moment)

87

GERI

Why do you live the way you do?

LYMAN

I'm fine.
    (Pause)
I eat okay, I sleep okay. I don't need nothing else. It don't matter what other people do—that's them, I'm me. I'm okay.

GERI

No. You're not okay at all.
    (Pause)

LYMAN

    (To GERI)
I held you in my arms. You wasn't any bigger than that. Not a week old.
    (A stunned silence. GERI looks to GENEVA, then back to LYMAN)
Every village over in Nam got a post in the middle for the spirits. They got genies all over, damn near every village. They do weird stuff. Your mother probably was one, I didn't know.

GERI

What was her name?

LYMAN

I heard it. I can't remember that language. She wasn't a kid like you said; she was older than us, she was twenty-five—thirty. She didn't come over here like you said. She stayed there.

GERI

She's still there?

88

Probably.
>   *(To GENEVA)*
You should have told her.

GENEVA

Geri's mother was described to us as a child fourteen
or fifteen. Geri's been told everything we know.

LYMAN

I bet I knew the girl your mother gave you to to bring
you over here. She was just some kid, wanted to come
to the States. Probably didn't give her right name. She
got twenty-five thousand dollars? She did okay.
>   *(Beat)*
I didn't sign no papers to bring her over here. They
shouldn't of used my name.

GERI

Are you my father?

LYMAN

No, ma'am, I'm not.

GERI

But you know who he is.

LYMAN

They shouldn't of used my name without telling me.

GERI

Why did they, then?

LYMAN

'Cause of the eyes probably. Made them think of it. I
don't think you inherit eyes like a husky dog, you're

just born with them. Freak of nature. Never did me any good.

I don't want to tell you people things you shouldn't know. It don't matter.

GERI

It matters, damnit. It matters a hell of a lot to me.

LYMAN

What do you care where you came from? You know who you are. You're who you are. You're okay. You're almost grown up.

GERI

I will turn you into a green jumping toad. I'm not joking.

GENEVA

Geri, don't say that. Actually, I don't think she could. Those things she does have to be beneficial to someone. Some of the kids wanted to get out of a history class early, Geri caused a total solar eclipse. Only the kids in her room saw it. Caused an enormous confusion. The teacher wouldn't even talk about it after a while.

Am I to understand that you knew Geri's parents in Vietnam?

LYMAN

Yes, ma'am. I didn't think so at first, except for the flower shop.

GENEVA

And you're not claiming to be her father.

LYMAN

No, ma'am.

GENEVA

But you think you know who he is.

LYMAN

Some things I can remember, some things I don't. Yeah,
I know.

GENEVA

You can pick one child out of forty thousand orphans
and recognize her sixteen years later.

LYMAN

(To GERI)
What did you say the odds was?

GERI

One in ten million. Same as the lottery.

LYMAN

They was worried about your eyes.

GERI

They're fine.

LYMAN

I tried to tell 'em. They was hysterical about it.

GENEVA

You're both driving me crazy.

LYMAN

Nobody knew your mother was going to have a kid. She
wasn't much bigger than you, but you couldn't tell. She
was a stylish woman. She was like the women over there
are, the ones with a little money, they're like you think
Frenchwomen would be. She got pregnant, she started
wearing those big coats they wear and all.

91

(Beat)

Your dad wanted you and him and your mother to live over there, but they wouldn't let him stay. He was all torn up.

(Beat)

He felt things too much, got depressed all the time. Lay around, mope around, saddest man I ever knew.

(Pause. He is reluctant to go on)

He loved you a lot. He was real proud. Some of us was in town, he had us come in the back of the flower shop and showed you to us. We passed you around. He was real proud. He couldn't bring her over here, he already had a wife in the States. But he had to keep you.

GERI

Why didn't he?

LYMAN

He did.

(Pause)

He was okay. He had the strongest hands of any man I ever shook hands with. He was gonna fix it up with the adoption people. So I guess that's what he did.

GENEVA

Oh, dear sweet God.

LYMAN

Looks like he'd of told you.

GENEVA

No. He could never have hurt Julia. He couldn't have told any of us, she'd have guessed.

GERI

Laird?

GENEVA

Of course.

GERI

You knew?

GENEVA

No.
        (To LYMAN)
He was in love with her. With Geri's mother, wasn't
he?

LYMAN

Yes, ma'am.

GENEVA

And he was fine till he found out he couldn't stay there.
We've never known why he changed—he became
so . . .

GERI

You're right, Lyman, he was the saddest man I've ever
known.

LYMAN

You didn't want to know, maybe you'll learn to leave
people alone. He was okay, but he had no business using
my name.

GERI

You don't remember my mother's name?

LYMAN

No, ma'am.

GERI

She couldn't keep me there? What, was she afraid she'd lose the business?

LYMAN

You want people to be perfect? People ain't perfect.

GERI

Laird. Good lord.

And I thought I was joking when I said to follow in my father's footsteps I had to mope and pine and drink myself to death. Not a very promising path he's laid out for me to follow.

GENEVA

You didn't really know him; he wasn't like that before the war.

LYMAN

He didn't drink. Over there he didn't drink.

GERI

What did he do?

LYMAN

He played the piano.
    (A pause)

GERI

He was a hell of a teacher.

GENEVA

Are you all right?

GERI

I told you my mother had a flower shop.

94

I could go with you. To Vietnam. We could think of
something. I mean, we could go to, I don't know, you
could tour Japan again, as much as you don't like it,
and we could go from there.

GERI

Vietnam is hardly a place you drop in on.

GENEVA

I have friends in Australia. You've never played Sydney.
You've needed someone to manage you since Laird.
God knows I have the time.

GERI

He played the piano.

GENEVA

Julia gets no kick out of touring with you and I love it,
so—

GERI

Julia!

GENEVA

Oh, good lord, Julia! She'll never be able to take it,
Geri.

GERI

We won't tell her.
     (Both at once notice LYMAN is no longer there)
Lyman! Lyman!

GENEVA

Mr. Fellers! Mr. Fellers!
     *(GERI runs off and back and off the other way,
     looking for him)*

GERI

Where the hell did he go? Ly-man!

GENEVA

Mr. Fellers! Geri, get him back.

GERI

(Calling at the top of her voice)

Yaw-hi toy ong traw lie taw!!

(The wind blows, kicking up a dust, the sky dark-ens, there is a stroke of lightning and a clap of thunder)

YAW-HI TOY ONG TRAW LIE TAW! HI MANN KONN CHAW KOO ONG DUN TAW! DUN DAY ONG TOAT!*

GENEVA

Mr. Fellers!

(In a second stroke of lightning we can see that LYMAN is back. The wind abates but it is still dark)

LYMAN

I don't know no more. I don't know things.

GERI

I don't care.

(The sky clears some. A dim setting sun slants hor-izontally through the trees)

LYMAN

I didn't ask you to talk to me; I don't want people talking to me. I don't know how to be with people. Don't expect things from me. I got nothing for you. I got nothing for you.

[* Wind—blow him back to me. Bring his dog to me. Don't let him get away!]

GERI

(Soothing)

I know.

LYMAN

He wanted to die, he died, let him die.

GERI

Nobody ever dies in my culture. You're always there.

LYMAN

Don't talk to me anymore. I don't know nothing more
about him.

GERI

I don't worry about Laird anymore.

LYMAN

I don't know how to talk to people. I don't know how
to be with people.

GERI

(She takes his hand)

You have a very strong constitution. You're very healthy
to spend so much time exposed to the elements. They've
been good to you.

LYMAN

I don't want nothing from you.

GERI

One of the first pieces Laird taught me was a piece I'd
like to play for you. You probably heard him play it. It
was one of his favorites. Maybe because he said he was
related to the composer. If that's true, then I guess I'm
related to him, too. His name was Erik-Alfred-Leslie

Satie; he was the spiritual godfather of *les six* in Paris. He wrote a piece as he imagined the gymnasts, back in Greece, had done their exercises to, when they were preparing for the Olympics. Daddy liked the idea of a girl playing it because women weren't allowed to watch the original Olympics. The athletes performed naked.

> *(She continues to hold his hand and raises her other arm in the air.*
>
> *The set slowly begins to return to the music room. They will be standing in the doorway when the change is complete)*

Any woman who saw them, even accidentally, was immediately put to death. You have to imagine the naked men, all very serious, standing on a green hill performing a series of exercises that look almost like a dance; very slowly in time to the music. They have incredible concentration, and they all move together in perfect synchronization.

> *She has let go of his hand. He remains standing in the doorway, watching her.*
>
> GENEVA *watches as* GERI *moves to the piano and begins to play the slow, steady* Gymnopédies *by Satie.*
>
> *After a long moment, as she plays, concentrating completely on her work,* LYMAN *moves a few steps into the room and sits on one of the straight-back chairs, watching her play.*

CURTAIN